Goody O'Grumpity

GOODY O'GRUMPITY

By Carol Ryrie Brink

Illustrated by

Ashley Wolff

North-South Books

NEW YORK · LONDON

ILLUSTRATOR'S NOTE

When I decided to illustrate Carol Ryrie Brink's wonderful poem, *Goody O'Grumpity,* the first thing I needed to do was figure out who Goody was. What did she look like? Where did she live? When did she live? My first clue came from her name. I knew that it was a custom in early America to call a married woman "goodwife", so perhaps Goody was a shortened term of endearment. I also suspected that the specific ingredients for Goody's cake mentioned in the text might be from an actual recipe.

My hunches were confirmed during a visit to Plymouth Plantation, in Plymouth, Massachusetts. I want to thank the staff at Plymouth for their help in my research, particularly Kathleen Curtin, the foodways manager, who supplied the seventeenth century spice cake recipe used as the basis for the recipe at the end of this book.

Although I can't be certain of Carol Ryrie Brink's intentions, I'd like to think she would be happy with my vision of Goody as a strong Pilgrim woman.

For Judy Sue **A.W.**

Text copyright © 1937, renewed 1964
Used by permission of the Estate of Carol Ryrie Brink
Illustrations copyright © 1994 by Ashley Wolff

Library of Congress Cataloging-in-Publication Data
Brink, Carol Ryrie. 1895-1981
Goody O'Grumpity / by Carol Ryrie Brink ; illustrated by Ashley Wolff.
Summary: Children come from far and near to taste
Goody O'Grumpity's wonderful spice cake.
ISBN 1-55858-327-0 (TRADE BINDING)
ISBN 1-55858-328-9 (LIBRARY BINDING)
[1. Baking—Fiction. 2. Stories in rhyme.] I. Wolff, Ashley, ill. II. Title
PZ8.3.B773GO 1994
[E]—DC20 94-5103

British Library Cataloguing in Publication Data is available

The art consists of linoleum block prints painted with watercolors.
Typography by Marc Cheshire / Printed in Belgium
1 3 5 7 9 TB 10 8 6 4 2
1 3 5 7 9 LB 10 8 6 4 2

W<small>HEN</small> Goody O'Grumpity

baked a cake

The tall reeds danced
by the mournful lake,
The pigs came nuzzling
out of their pens,

The dogs ran sniffing
and so did the hens,

And the children flocked
by dozens and tens.
They came from the north,
the east and the south
With wishful eyes
and watering mouth,

And stood in a crowd
about Goody's door,
Their muddy feet
on her sanded floor.
And what do you s'pose
they came to do!

Why, to lick the dish
when Goody was through!

And throughout the land
went such a smell
Of citron and spice—
no words can tell

How cinnamon bark
and lemon rind,
And round, brown nutmegs
grated fine

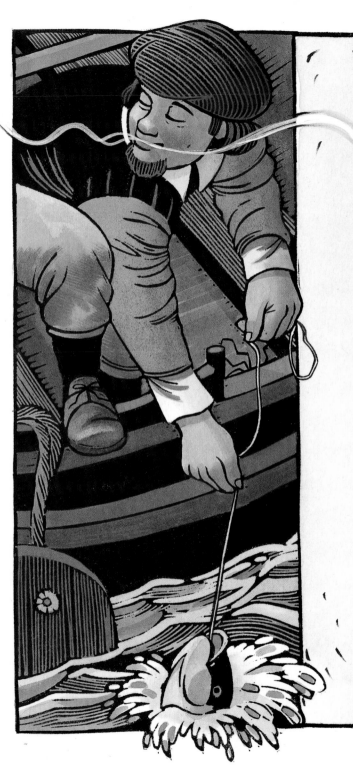

A wonderful haunting
perfume wove,
Together with allspice,
ginger and clove,

When Goody but opened
the door of her stove.

The children moved close
in a narrowing ring,
They were hungry—as hungry
as bears in the spring;

They said not a word,
just breathed in the spice,
And at last when the cake
was all golden and nice,
Goody took a great knife
and cut each a slice.

¾ cup milk
½ cup butter
2 teaspoons salt
¾ cup sugar
1 tablespoon active dry yeast
3 eggs
1 teaspoon grated lemon rind
1½ teaspoon cinnamon
¼ teaspoon grated nutmeg
½ teaspoon allspice
¼ teaspoon ground ginger
¼ teaspoon ground cloves
2½ cups unbleached all-purpose flour
2½ cups whole wheat flour plus more
for kneading
¼ cup diced citron
1 cup currants

GOODY O'GRUMPITY'S SPICE CAKE

Makes 2 loaves

•

SAFETY FIRST!
*Children should be supervised
carefully by an adult when
making this recipe.*

1. Bring the milk to a boil in a small saucepan. Stir in the butter, salt and sugar. Set aside and let cool until lukewarm.

2. In a medium bowl, stir the yeast into ½ cup lukewarm water until thoroughly dissolved. Stir in the milk mixture and then the eggs, lemon rind, cinnamon, nutmeg, allspice, ginger, and cloves. Stir in the unbleached flour and 2½ cups of the whole wheat flour. Turn out the dough onto a board heavily dusted with whole wheat flour. Knead until smooth and resilient, about 5 minutes, adding more whole wheat flour if necessary. Cover with plastic wrap and set aside for ½ hour in a warm place.

3. Knead in the citron and currants.

4. Place the dough in a large bowl, cover with plastic wrap, and allow to rise until doubled in bulk, about 1 hour.

5. Punch down the dough, divide in two, and form into round loaves. Set these on a cookie sheet, cover loosely, and allow to rise until doubled, about 1 hour more.

6. Preheat oven to 300°F.

7. Bake for about 1½-2 hours. Test for doneness by tapping the bottom of a loaf: it is fully baked if it sounds hollow.